Paral of Light

(Special Edition)

Bringing Light to a Troubled Sea

by

Barbara Davis

Bringing Light to a Troubled Sea   Barbara Davis

First printing

Revival Waves of Glory has allowed this work to remain exactly as the author intended, verbatim, without editorial input.

Unless otherwise noted Scripture quotations have been taken from The Holy Bible, King James Version.

Ebook 978-1-312-59727-3
Softcover 978-0692344200
Hardcover 978-1-312-59726-6

PUBLISHED BY REVIVAL WAVES OF GLORY BOOKS & PUBLISHING
www.revivalwavesofglory.com
Litchfield, IL

Published in the United States of America

Special Thanks

Special thanks to Lilly Losh, my dear and trusted friend, whose prayers help, and encouragement has meant more to me than she knows.   Special thanks to my pastors, Pastor Cora Lee and Leonard Barber, and to my brothers and sisters at Communion Church. Special thanks also to Christi Checkett and Jackie Money who have been a blessing from God and to my family.

Dedication

I dedicate this book to the Lord Jesus Christ and to my sons Oscar and Robert.

Barbara Davis

Dedication
In Loving Memory of Barbara Davis

Barbara Davis's book was one of the first books published through Revival Waves of Glory Books & Publishing. She was a fresh breath of life with a pure spirit. You will be missed but your words will live on.

Bill Vincent / President
Revival Waves of Glory Books & Publishing

I am writing in remembrance of a dear and very special woman of God, that the Lord Himself hand chose to put in my life as an intercessor, voice of wisdom, and to be my spiritual mom in the truest sense of the word. I had the awesome pleasure of meeting Ms. Barbara in 2001. She has literally been in my life ever sense as all of the above. So many times she shared her visions and dreams with me, and the insight that the Lord had given her concerning them - Not knowing that one day they would be put into an inspiring book of encouragement to seek the Lord; and know that he is showing you something - that he wants to reveal a facet of himself or give a glimpse of His vast knowledge. After hearing the visions over the years and their interpretations , when I read the book what blessed me was the scriptures that the Holy Spirit gave her for each vision. You just know that it is from the Lord. I would like to end by leaving this with the reader of Parables of Light: This woman of God, Ms. Barbara Davis is the true deal. She loved the Lord Jesus Christ with all her heart, and was truly a woman of prayer. It was holiness or nothing. This world had nothing to offer her at all. I love and thank God for putting her in my life for a covenant relationship. Love Sheila, your spiritual daughter.

Sheila Berry

Barbara would "hug" us with her smile...her eyes. Her prayers wrapped us in love.

Lyn Asta

I was blessed to have known Barbara as a friend, partner in ministry and true woman of God. I miss you dearly Barbara.

Lillie Losh

For where two or three are assembled together in My name, there I am also among them. Matthew 18:20 (Hebraic Roots Bible). When Barbara was among those gathered together, you knew the Lord was there also.

Bill Losh

Barbara has been one of my closest friends for over fifteen years. During this time I have always been inspired with her sincere commitment and intimate daily walk with Christ. Her faithfulness and perseverance in meditation and prayer, and her tenacity to search out books whose authors were of great godly integrity was always impressive.

She has been a loyal friend and an incredible source of strength and encouragement to myself and family. I shall ever be grateful to her loyalty and warm and comforting kindness.

I trust that this inspiring book will enlighten the hearts of many and that the Father will subdue our inner man as He unfolds His deep and secret revelations in this troubled world of gross obscurity.

Elsie M. Garner
Member of Communion Church Ministries

To my best friend and confidant. Thanks for sharing your relationship with the Father, Jesus and the Holy Spirit with us. This book have touch my life in a great way. When I read this book I will always have your smile your heart and your Love with me. When people read this book through the eyes of the their spirit they will surely see the Love of the Father for them. I miss you much.

Love, your Sis in Christ
Robin Collins

Barbara Davis was my friend, a spiritual counselor, a prayer warrior for me since January, 2013. I have known Barbara a long time. But we really became friend and spiritual sister in 2013 when I started picking her up for prayer every day. Barbara helped me in my spiritual growth(to know the Father, Son and the Holy Spirit). She would said greater is He that inside you that is in the world. The Holy Spirit, He will teach you all things. And because of her, I began to study and meditate Gods words and through faith I received more revelations and knowledge about the spiritual things of God.

Barbara was an intercessor at Communion Church Ministries for many years. She came to prayer every day, Tuesday through Friday from 11:00-2:00 every week. When Barbara prayed the heavens were opened and

God answered every prayer. Many people were healed and delivery.

She revealed this by the dreams and vision she wrote about in her book (the Parables of Light.)

As the world reads Barbara book about the dreams and vision she had their lives will be changed. As they read the scriptures she gave, they will began to walk in love, peace, brotherly kindness, goodness, mercy and humidity. They will learn how to become a Bride of Christ. They will also learn how to overcome fiery trails to be filled with joy from the glory of the

Lord. And above all things to take the shield of faith; to take the helmet of salvation and the sword of the spirit which is the word of God; praying always with all prayer supplication in the spirit (Ephesians 6:16-18.)

Sallye Johnson
Friend
St. Louis, MO

To our sister Barbara, we love you and you are deeply missed.

Your Sisters
Shirley and Buelah

Barbara was whatever we needed her to be in a time of need, she was our counsel, our mother, a friend, and definitely a prayer warrior for all. She represented "love", she will be greatly missed.

Rick and Cherry Jackson

To my best friend, confident. Thanks for sharing your relationship with The Father, Jesus and the Holy Spirit with us. This book has touch my life in a great way. When I read this book I will always have your smile your heart and your Love with me. when people read this book through the eyes of their spirit they will sure see the Love of the Father. I will miss your dearly.

Love your Sis in Christ
Robin Collins

Table of Content

Periscopic Imagination

Although a submarine is submerged under water, if one comes up high enough with a periscope, one can see into another realm.

So it is in the Spirit, if you come up high enough with the periscope of your imagination, you can see into the spiritual realm.

The Bike and the Motorcycle

The Lord gave me a vision of a bike and a motorcycle. Then He said that I needed to leave the bike behind and that it was time for me to advance in my walk with Him. The bike had been instrumental in getting me to this point but now it was time for the Power of the Motorcycle.

Hebrews 6:1-3 [Amplified]

Therefore let us go on and get past the elementary stage in the teachings and doctrine of Christ (the Messiah), advancing steadily toward the completeness and perfection that belong to spiritual maturity. Let us not again be laying the foundation of repentance and abandonment of dead works (dead formalism) and of the faith [by which you turned] to God,

2 With teachings about purifying, the laying on of hands, the resurrection from the dead, and eternal judgment and punishment. [These are all matters of which you should have been fully aware long, long ago.]

3 If indeed God permits, we will [now] proceed [to advanced teaching].

A Whole Lot of Shaking Going On

I saw a huge elephant running, but he was running with a purpose. Things were being shaken and thrown off course and there was great disturbance in the spiritual realm.

Now the enemy didn't like this, but there was nothing he could do about it because the elephant was on a mission from God and all he had to do was run. So every now and then I see myself as that elephant running in the Spirit just to shake up the enemy's plans.

Those who sing should sing songs to the glory of God. Musicians should play, dancers should dance. Whatever your gift is do it to the glory of the Lord and let's shake up some things in the enemy's camp. Amen!

Acts 16:25

And at midnight Paul and Silas prayed, and sang praises unto God: and the prisoners heard them.

Acts 16:26

And suddenly there was a great earthquake, so that the foundations of the prison were shaken: and immediately all the doors were opened, and every one's bands were loosed.

Spit in Your Eyes

I had a vision in which the Lord Jesus spit and rubbed it in my eyes. Remembering the blind man in Mark 8:25, that He did the same thing too, I asked, "Does this mean I can't see?"

He answered and said, "This means that I am opening and anointing your spiritual eyes to see further than they ever have before."

2 Kings 6:17

And Elisha prayed, and said, LORD, I pray thee, open his eyes, that he may see. And the LORD opened the eyes of the young man; and he saw: and, behold, the mountain was full of horses and chariots of fire round about Elisha.

Talitha Cumi
(The Real Me)

Once, while having a discussion with someone, I found myself becoming very defensive and began acting in a way that is not becoming for a Christian. Afterwards the Lord spoke to me and said, "Barbara that is not you."

And I thought it's not? because I meant every word that I said

But the Lord said, "No it is not. You have played so many different roles in your life that you have lost sight of who you really are."

Then He said to me, "Let me show you, you."

Then we took a trip through what may have been my soul and I saw all of the different roles I had played in my life. None of the which were the real me. We walked over to what appeared to be a corner of my soul and there was this little frightened girl. Then the Lord said, "That is the real you."

I was shocked. Then, the Lord picked up the little girl and He hugged her. I felt myself begin to grow up quickly. As I grew I started to learn things about myself and I started to like this girl. She's been hidden a long time, but is coming out strong in the Lord. And I am finding out that I like myself better than any of the other roles I've ever played.

St. Mark 5:41

And he took the damsel by the hand, and said unto her, Talitha cumi; which is, being interpreted, Damsel, I say unto thee, arise.

16

The Sword and the Scepter

In a vision, I saw the Lord Jesus with a gold crown, now the crown was alive! The inside was made of a thick blood red material, and the outside was like clear gold with all of the names of the fruit of the sprit written upon it. The names were alive, and moving all over the crown with light emanating from them.

Then the Lord placed the crown on my head and it fit perfectly. It was absolutely amazing. It was the crown of Life! Then He placed a sword in one hand and a scepter in the other and said, "In order to walk in kingly authority and fight the good fight of faith, you must have the fruit of the Spirit alive and active in your life."

Galatians 5:22 -23a

But the fruit of the Spirit is love, joy, peace, longsuffering, gentleness, goodness, faith, Meekness, temperance:

The Kaleidoscopic Word of God

The Lord revealed to me that - just as the kaleidoscope has bits of glass that are reflected by mirrors, so that when the tube is turned, beautiful colors, images and patterns appear and are changed with each rotation of the tube. So it is with the Word of God. As we go deep into The Word and search out its true riches, it changes, and we are changed by it. The deeper we go it continues to change and continues to change us.

II Corinthians 3:18

But we all, with open face beholding as in a glass the glory of the Lord, are changed into the same image from glory to glory, even as by the Spirit of the Lord.

18

Talking Tears

I was in the Spirit and had a vision in which I saw an unusual looking door. Over the top of the door I saw in a moment of time written in every language the word **Private**. Then, the door opened and I looked inside and saw a throne and beautiful crystal bottles as far as the eye could see. Inside the bottle were tears. These tears were talking, telling of sorrows, joys, ecstasies, and adorations that had no human words or expressions, and the only person who could understand the tears was God Himself. That is when He spoke and said, "When all you can do is cry – cry – because what you can't say; your tears are talking for you."

Psalm 56:8b

Put thou my tears into thy bottle: are they not in thy book?

St. John 11:35

Jesus wept.

The Jay Walker

Once, in a vision, I saw a woman crossing a very busy street, but, she was jay walking and before she knew it danger was upon her. Then the Lord spoke and said, "Always follow the signals and warnings given to you by the Holy Spirit, even if there may seem a shorter way to get to your desired destination. Because He knows the pitfalls, dangers and distractions that could wind up costing you a lot more than just a few steps."

Proverbs 14:12 Amplified

There is a way which seems right to a man *and* appears straight before him, but at the end of it is the way of death.

Isaiah 30:21

And your ears will hear a word behind you, saying, This is the way; walk in it, when you turn to the right hand and when you turn to the left

Walking on Nothing

In a vision I saw Jesus leaning against this marble structure with His feet crossed and His arms folded across His chest. Then with two fingers He beckoned me to come. But as I got closer He leaped over the side into this beautiful garden and told me to jump, which I did. Then we began to walk through the garden to a gate. Now Jesus did all the talking. I did not say a word because I could see that beyond the gate there was nothing. When we got to the gate He stepped out, but I stood still. He said, "Come on, Barbara."

I said, "There is nothing there for me to walk on."

He said again, "Come on."

So I stepped out cautiously and began to walk with Him. Now, as I was walking, land appeared under my feet but only after I had made the first step. So we walked on, but I kept thinking what if I miss a step and fall? I better go back. And as I turned, I saw this beautiful land behind me but I could barely see the garden anymore. Then the Lord spoke and said, "If you go back now all of the progress that you've made thus far will disappear and you will fall before you make it to the garden, besides do you really want to go back after having made all of this progress and come all this way?" Then the vision ended.

Now after some time had passed and I had gone through a trial, I was given a dream in which I found myself in the same place as when the vision ended. There was still nothing in front of us, only this time, I am in front of Jesus walking backward! Now I am doing all of the talking, land is still appearing under my feet with each step. But this time I am not afraid and there is a smile on Jesus' face.

Then I noticed that he began to look beyond me. So I turned around and there is this huge majestic mountain with thrones on it. Then the Lord sat on one and I sat on the one next to Him. When I looked out over the land I saw lots of people running and sitting on thrones too! Then the Lord spoke and said, "Barbara, dare to do what no one has done before!"

St. Matthew 14:28

And Peter answered him and said, Lord, if it be thou, bid me come unto thee on the water.

St. Matthew 14:29

And he said, Come. And when Peter was come down out of the ship, he walked on the water, to go to Jesus.

Eyes That Hear and Ears That See

The Lord spoke to me and said, "Deception has come upon the world and you'll have to comprehend by the Spirit. Sometimes what you see, you'll have to understand by listening in the Spirit, and what you'll hear by seeing in the Spirit."

"So, have eyes that hear and ears that see by the Spirit."

I Corinthians 2:12a [Amplified]

Now we have not received the spirit [that belongs to] the world, but the [Holy] Spirit Who is from God,

I Corinthians 2:13 [Amplified]

And we are setting these truths forth in words not taught by human wisdom but taught by the [Holy] Spirit, combining *and* interpreting spiritual truths with spiritual language [to those who possess the Holy Spirit].

I Corinthians 2:14 [Amplified]

But the natural, nonspiritual man does not accept *or* welcome *or* admit into his heart the gifts *and* teachings *and* revelations of the Spirit of God, for they are folly (meaningless nonsense) to him; and he is incapable of knowing them [of progressively recognizing, understanding, and becoming better acquainted with them] because they are spiritually discerned *and* estimated *and* appreciated.

The Path of the Elephant

Once in a vision the Lord revealed me as an elephant in the wilderness making a path for other elephants. I was paving the way so that their journey would not be as hard, and so they wouldn't make the same mistakes as I had made. They would learn by doing what they saw me do and it wouldn't take them as long to make it here. Then, some started to move out on their own, paving a way for others. Then, I heard the Lord say, "Well done."

St. Matthew 23:13

But woe unto you, scribes and Pharisees, hypocrites! for ye shut up the kingdom of heaven against men: for ye neither go in yourselves, neither suffer ye them that are entering to go in

St. Luke 11:52a

Woe unto you, lawyers! for ye have taken away the key of knowledge

St. Matthew 5:19b

but whosoever shall do and teach them, the same shall be called great in the kingdom of heaven.

Going Up Backwards

I saw a pair of feet on a stairway that appeared to be going downward. The Lord asked me a question, "Are the feet going down forward or up backward?"

I thought, I don't know.

So He said, "Barbara, there will be times that I'll ask you to come up backward. Sometimes it will be for your benefit and other times to let you know if you trust Me in certain areas. In any case I'd rather have you always coming up than going down."

Then He said, "You have to learn to trust me, even when things seem to be going backward."

Proverbs 3:5

Trust in the LORD with all thine heart; and lean not unto thine own understanding

The Husbandman

While asking the Lord to forgive me for something that I had done wrong, I had a vision in which I saw the Father dressed as a gardener and working in a garden. There was a wheel barrow and gardening tools and little animals were all around, watching Him work.

Then I asked, "What are you doing, Lord?"

He answered, "Purging and taking away." He continued, "As long as you confess your sins and shortcomings you allow me to do the work needful to keep the garden growing and producing, and as long as you do your part, then, I will do mine."

Then He said in a caring and tentative voice, "I am the Husbandman."

Saint John 15:1-2

I am the true vine, and my Father is the husbandman. Every branch in me that beareth not fruit he taketh away: and every branch that beareth fruit, he purgeth it, that it may bring forth more fruit.

Here Comes the Bride

There was a beautiful wedding at a church near where I lived and I watched as the limousines pulled up and the wedding party got out. Everyone looked nice and the guests were so happy as they all went inside the church.

Then the bride pulled up! Oh my, she looked so beautiful in her white gown surrounded by all her bridesmaids. I continued to watch until they all went inside the church and the doors closed. After the wedding was over and the guests were gone, I sat down to study the Word when I heard a lot of commotion outside my bedroom window.

Then the Lord spoke and said, "Get up and go look out the window." So I did and to my horror there was the bride in her white gown with a drink in one hand and a beer in the other, dancing provocatively. And the cars driving by were honking their horns and giving her the thumbs up. The people walking by were clapping and cheering her on.

Then the Lord said in a lamentum voice, "She is indicative of my Bride today. She comes to church, uses my name for a show and pretends she is married to me. But, afterwards she does these abominations and greater. As I watched her I wept and prayed for the bride of Christ.

Isaiah 4:1

And in that day seven women shall take hold of one man, saying, we will eat our own bread, and wear our own apparel: only let us be called by thy name, to take away our reproach.

St. John 11:35

Jesus wept.

Spoiled Vines

I saw in a vision a man dressed in a glorious robe and powerful in the things that pertained to the kingdom. But about his neck he wrestled with a very small demon. This man had done great things. So I asked God, "What is this and what does it mean?"

He answered and said, "There is an area in his life that he has not dealt with which leaves a door open and makes him vulnerable to this small demon who torments him and he is too ashamed and afraid to bring it to me so that my Grace can free him. But if he doesn't, he will never walk in the fullness of all that I have for him and he is in danger of losing what he has now." Then He said, "It's the little foxes that spoil the vine."

Saddened, I watched as that little demon took away from all that glory.

Song of Solomon 2:15a

Take us the foxes, the little foxes, that spoil the vines:

The Mandate and the Badge

While sitting in my chair, the Lord spoke and said, "There is a mandate on your life for this time and season." Then He showed me a gold badge, shaped like a police officer's badge."

So, I looked up the word mandate and it is defined as: an authorization to act given to a representative. A badge is: an emblem worn to show rank or status.

Then He said, "I am passing out badges to those who qualify."

St. Mark 6:7

And He called to Him the Twelve [apostles] and began to send them out [as His ambassadors] two by two and gave them authority *and* power over the unclean spirits

Luke 10:19 [Amplified]

Behold! I have given you authority *and* power to trample upon serpents and scorpions, and [physical and mental strength and ability] over all the power that the enemy [possesses]; and nothing shall in any way harm you.

When Prayers Change, Men Will Change

Once, while in prayer, the Lord revealed this to me. This is how you pray, "Oh, Lord, deliver me from the thief. Oh Lord, deliver me from the rapist. Oh Lord, deliver me from the murderer. But I want you to learn to pray for the thief, rapist and the murderer. Because when prayers change, men will change."

I Timothy 2:3

For this is good and acceptable in the sight of God our Saviour;

I Timothy 2:4

Who will have all men to be saved, and to come unto the knowledge of the truth.

The Two Trunks

I was in prayer, the Lord spoke and said, "I am going to show you – you – in the Spirit." Then suddenly there face to face with me was an elephant. I was outdone because I couldn't think of anything about an elephant that anyone would desire to be. So I got up off my knees and I didn't tell anyone about this vision – not even my pastor, who at the time I shared a lot of my dreams and visions with, and who also had suggested that I get the tapes on dreams and visions by John Paul Jackson which I did.   And in them, to my surprise, he spoke about the elephant and said that the elephant is a symbol of wisdom and strength.

So, needless to say, after hearing this, that I went running back to the Lord saying, "OK Lord, I will be an elephant."

But God wasn't finished with the vision yet. In the next part of the vision I saw an elephant standing beside a tree, then my focus zoomed in on the trunks of the elephant and the tree. Then this huge axe came out of nowhere and severed both of the trunks. Horrified, I screamed, "What does this mean?"

Then the Lord answered, "If you sever either one of these from their source, which are their trunks, they will die." Then He said, "I am your source, you must stay connected to Me!"

St. John 15:4

Abide in me, and I in you. As the branch cannot bear fruit of itself, except it abide in the vine; no more can ye, except ye abide in me.

Peripheral Vision

I awoke from a dream hearing the words 'peripheral vision'. So I asked the Lord, "What do the words mean?"

He answered, "Peripheral vision belongs to the watchmen. They catch things out of the corner of their eyes. They can discern what sort of spirit it is and its mission. The watchmen can see what others miss, then pray for and or warn those to whom they have been assigned."

Then He said, "I have given you peripheral vision."

Isaiah 21:6

For thus hath the LORD said unto me, Go, set a watchman, let him declare what he seeth.

Oh, If Men Would but Pray

While I was praying and interceding for others, I saw in the Spirit a huge magnet suspended over the earth. And when I prayed against the things that were not in accordance with the will of God for their lives the magnet would draw them. And when I looked again at the magnet I saw all of the unholy works of darkness on it.

Then, I heard the voice of the Lord say, "Oh, if Men Would but Pray."

Ephesians 6:18

Praying always with all prayer and supplication in the Spirit, and watching thereunto with all perseverance and supplication for all saints;

Colossians 4:2

Continue in prayer, and watch in the same with thanksgiving

James 5:16b

The effectual fervent prayer of a righteous man availeth much.

The Two Thieves

I saw in a vision a man lying against a pillar and on top of the pillar was a beautiful crown. Now the crown belonged to the man, but he acted as if this did not matter. He just laid there lazily with a piece of straw in his mouth, watching the world go by.

Then the Lord asked me a question: "Which thief do you think will overtake him?"

I said, "I don't know."

He answered, "Both!"

St. John 10:10

The thief cometh not but for to steal, to kill and to destroy.

Revelation 3:3

If therefore thou shalt not watch, I will come on thee as a thief, and thou shalt not know what hour I will come upon thee.

Revelation 16:15a

Behold, I come as a thief.

The Gifts

While in the Spirit the Lord spoke and said, "Wrap up Love, Peace, Brotherly Kindness, Goodness and Mercy. Seal them with a smile and pass them out as gifts from me.

Colossians 3:12

Put on therefore, as the elect of God, holy and beloved, bowels of mercies, kindness, humbleness of mind, meekness, longsuffering

Romans 12:10

Be kindly affectioned one to another with brotherly love; in honour preferring one another

Ephesians 4:32a

And be ye kind one to another, tenderhearted, forgiving one another, even as God for Christ's sake hath forgiven you.

I Thessalonians 4:9

But as touching brotherly love ye need not that I write unto you: for ye yourselves are taught of God to love one another

The Beautiful Serene Picture

Once while looking on the back of a cereal box, there was this chaotic picture. Now, you were supposed to locate a beautiful serene picture inside of this chaotic one. I looked for the picture this way and that way, upside down and downside up. It took awhile but as I looked harder – WOW! Right before my eyes the picture jumped out at me.

Then the Lord spoke, "Sometimes it may seem as if your life is in chaos – one thing after another, but believe me, right in the midst of your chaos I am creating something beautiful and serene.'

I Peter 4:12 - 13

Beloved, think it not strange concerning the fiery trial which is to try you, as though some strange thing happened unto you: But rejoice, inasmuch as ye are partakers of Christ's sufferings; that, when his glory shall be revealed, ye may be glad also with exceeding joy.

I Peter 5:10

But the God of all grace, who hath called us unto his eternal glory by Christ Jesus, after that ye have suffered a while, make you perfect, establish, strengthen, settle you.

The Broken Clock

The Lord showed me a huge clock, but it was not a regular clock. This clock looked different. I had never seen anything quite like it before. Then I saw the foot of the Lord step on and break the clock. So I asked, "What does this mean?"

He answered and said, "The reason the clock looked different to you is because it was not a clock of time as you know it but this clock was of dispensations of times and ages."

Then He said, "The reason why I stepped on it and broke it is because it had served its purpose and that those times will never be again. We have entered into another era; The End Time Era."

Isaiah 42:9

Behold, the former things are come to pass, and new things do I declare:

Isaiah 48:7

They are created now, and not from the beginning; even before the day when thou heardest them not; lest thou shouldest say, Behold, I knew them.

Jeremiah 30:7a [Amplified]

Alas! for that day will be great, so that none will be like it; it will be the time of Jacob's [unequaled] trouble,

Fishing Poles and Eagle's Wings

I saw a fishing pole with two eagle's wings on it. I asked the Lord, "What does this mean?"

He answered, "The fish that are being caught in these end times will mature very quickly, in some cases, quicker than the fishermen, because the time is short and my return is near."

Fish represent people.

Fishing poles symbolizes salvation.

Eagle's wings symbolize maturity in spiritual things.

Isaiah 66:7

Before she travailed, she brought forth; before her pain came, she was delivered of a man child.

Amos 9:13a

Behold, the days come, saith the LORD, that the plowman shall overtake the reaper, and the treader of grapes him that soweth seed;

The Three Ring Circus

I had a dream in which I saw a three ring circus and there were lots of spectacular things going on: tight rope acts, clowns, magicians, horses, and elephants – just all kinds of stuff. There was also a ringmaster with a bull horn who kept the people happy and held their attention with the sensationalism.

But, pushed way in the back, hanging on the cross, bleeding and dying was Jesus. If anyone would look over at Him the ringmaster would make light of it, as if it were of no significance and grab their attention again.

Then, the Lord spoke and said, "These are the things that are happening in the churches today – all types of nonsense that have nothing to do with godliness or pure holiness and the true gospel is being pushed further and further away."

Isaiah 30:9

This a rebellious people, lying children, children that will not hear the law of Lord.

Isaiah 30:10

Which say to the seers, See not; and to the prophets, Prophesy not unto us right things, speak unto us smooth things, prophesy deceits:

Isaiah 30:11

Get you out of the way, turn aside out of the path, cause the Holy One of Israel to cease from before us.

2 Timothy 4:3

For the time will come when they will not endure sound doctrine; but after their own lusts shall they heap to themselves teachers, having itching ears;

2 Timothy 4:4a

And they shall turn away their ears from the truth

Jeremiah 5:30 -31a

A wonderful and horrible thing is committed in the land; the prophets prophesy falsely, and the priests bear rule by their means; and my people love to have it so:

Deep Calleth Unto Deep

In a dream I saw myself on a sea shore jumping in and out of shallow water when I heard a voice say, "Go deep." So, I began to go down deeper and deeper.

Then I heard another voice say, "You had better go back. You have never been this deep before," and I thought yeah I better go back. Then fear gripped me and I began to drown but a dolphin came and took me to the surface and I woke up. But the dream troubled me because I had gotten fearful.

Then the Lord spoke and said, "I knew you would become fearful and want to go back but this is just the beginning of the call for you to come deeper into me. Remember John Mark? He also gave up and went back. But while Paul and Barnabus contended over him I knew what I was creating in him and not only would he become profitable to Paul but to all who will read the gospel according to Mark."

Psalm 42:7

Deep calleth unto deep at the noise of thy waterspouts: all thy waves and thy billows are gone over me

The Effective Power
of Gentle Words

After hearing my pastor teach; and seeing the manner in which she flowed, I had a vision of a waterfall and saw how gently it flowed over the edge. But it hit the rocks below with such power and force that the water sprayed out in all directions. So were the words of her mouth, they flowed out with such gentle wisdom but hit with such effective power that I had the feeling when we left there that her words would be carried out in all directions.

Proverbs 18:4

The words of a [discreet and wise] man's mouth are like deep waters [plenteous and difficult to fathom], and the fountain of skillful *and* godly Wisdom is like a gushing stream [sparkling, fresh, pure, and life-giving].

Peek a Boo, I See You

The Lord Jesus pulled open my heart and said, "Peek inside." Now, I did not like everything that I saw, but the Lord assured me that this was not meant to condemn me. He wanted me to take a closer look at the things in my heart that were not pleasing to Him.

Now, I had been praying during this time and asking God to remove those things that were a hindrance to my walk with Him. We are working on those things and I know that I am growing – but – every now and then when I am not walking according to His way, I'll hear: "Peek a Boo, I See You."

Psalm 33:18

Behold, the eye of the LORD is upon them that fear him, upon them that hope in his mercy;
    Psalm 32:8

I will instruct thee and teach thee in the way which thou shalt go: I will guide thee with mine eye
Psalm 34:15a

The eyes of the LORD are upon the righteous,

Psalm 139:23

Search me, O God, and know my heart: try me, and know my thoughts:

Psalm 139:24

And see if there be any wicked way in me, and lead me in the way everlasting.

The Confirming Word of God

I saw in a vision my son walking toward me wearing an orange shirt. But the strange thing about the vision was that I saw the front and back of him at the same time in one body. I was so astonished! So I asked, "What does this mean Lord?"

He let me know that the color orange symbolizes a double anointing, and that my son would be blessed coming and going. I really wanted to share the vision and its meaning with my son but the Lord would not allow it. He just said, "This is not the time."

But in the year 2011 the Lord said, "The time is now. Call your son." So I called him and told him the vision and he said "Mama." And I said, "Yes." And again he said, "Mama!" And I said, "What?" Then he said, "It is ironic that you would call me now and say this because I am sitting here with an orange shirt on with two eyes on the back of it." And I thought with laughter, "Wow! God will confirm His word with signs; we just have to move in His timing. God waited until he had gotten the shirt, and then said, "Now call your son."

St. Mark 16:20b

And they went forth, and preached every where, the Lord working with them, and confirming the word with signs following

46

The Sword of the Word

I saw the Lord in a vision as a waterfall and in His hand was a sword. Now this was an unusual sword because it had the ability to cut through elements like water, wind, space and time and even darkness.

So, I asked the Lord, "What kind of a sword is this?"

And He answered saying, "This sword is for those who know the depth of the Word of God and who use it skillfully."

Ephesians 1:17b [Amplified]

that He may grant you a spirit of wisdom and revelation [of insight into mysteries and secrets] in the [deep and intimate] knowledge of Him,

Ephesians 1:18b [Amplified]

By having the eyes of your heart flooded with light, so that you can know *and* understand the hope to which He has called you

Ephesians 1:19a [Amplified]

And [so that you can know and understand] what is the immeasurable *and* unlimited *and* surpassing greatness of His power in *and* for us who believe

Darken Counsel

In a vision I saw a huge beautiful Bible suspended in mid-air. It was trimmed in gold and had jewels all over it. As I walked closer to it I could see that the edges of the pages were white. But when I looked inside, all the pages were black. Startled, I jumped back and asked the Lord, "What is this?"

He said, "Darken Counsel." I questioned Him about the meaning and He said, "This is the teachings, traditions, and doctrines of men who have changed the truth of God into a lie."

Job 38:2

Who is this that darkeneth counsel by words without knowledge?

St. Matthew 15:9

But in vain they do worship me, teaching for doctrines the commandments of men.

Romans 1:25

Who changed the truth of God into a lie, and worshipped and served the creature more than the Creator, who is blessed for ever. Amen.

Little Babies With Big Ideas

I saw in a vision what I thought was a baby in a high chair. Now this baby was having a tantrum – kicking and screaming to the top of its lungs. Then I saw these loving hands doing all they could for the child but still the child kicked and screamed.

As I got closer to the highchair, I would see that it was not a baby at all; it was a full grown person! So I asked the Lord, "What does this mean?"

He said, "My people say to me, 'Lord, Let me do something great for you or for the kingdom or let me minister to others'. As soon as I start to do the work that is needful for them to walk in these areas they throw a fit, but as long as they act like babies they shall be treated like babies."

I Corinthians 3: 1-2

And I, brethren, could not speak unto you as unto spiritual, but as unto carnal, even as unto babes in Christ. I have fed you with milk, and not with meat: for hitherto ye were not able to bear it, neither yet now are ye able.

Hebrews 5:12

For when for the time ye ought to be teachers, ye have need that one teach you again which be the first principles of the oracles of God; and are become such as have need of milk, and not of strong meat.

49

Hebrews 5:13

For every one that useth milk is unskilful in the word of righteousness: for he is a babe.

The Immature Man – Child

Once in a dream the Lord took me to the portals of hell and I saw children everywhere in torment. Amazed! I said, "Lord, they are just children!"

But He said, "No they are not, watch." So as I watched they were transformed into fully grown men and women. Then they turned back into crying, whining children. Then, the Lord said, "No matter how much I tried to reason with them, or warn them, or help them; they never wanted to mature or develop their spirit. So, children they were and children they shall remain throughout eternity."

I Corinthians 14:20 [Amplified]

Brethren, do not be children [immature] in your thinking; continue to be babes in [matters of] evil, but in your minds be mature [men].

I Corinthians 14:21 [Amplified]

It is written in the Law, By men of strange languages and by the lips of foreigners will I speak to this people, and not even then will they listen to Me, says the Lord.

I Corinthians 13:11 [Amplified]

When I was a child, I talked like a child, I thought like a child, I reasoned like a child; now that I have become a man, I am done with childish ways and have put them aside.

I Peter 2:2 [Amplified]

Like newborn babies you should crave (thirst for, earnestly desire) the pure (unadulterated) spiritual milk, that by it you may be nurtured and grow unto [completed] salvation,

I Peter 2:3 [Amplified]

Since you have [already] tasted the goodness and kindness of the Lord.

Simply Profound

I saw in a vision little children with gray hair and old eyes. They spoke of profound things with such clarity and simplicity that I was astonished! Then the Lord revealed to me that we have to listen and watch what our children are doing and saying in this hour, for they will speak and do profound things with such childlike simplicity that if you blink you just might miss it.

Psalm 8:2

Out of the mouth of babes and sucklings hast thou ordained strength because of thine enemies, that thou mightest still the enemy and the avenger

St. Matthew 21:16b

And Jesus saith unto them, Yea; have ye never read, Out of the mouth of babes and sucklings thou hast perfected praise

St. Matthew 19:14

But Jesus said, Suffer little children, and forbid them not, to come unto me: for of such is the kingdom of heaven.

Fresh Manna or Old Stale Bread

The Lord revealed to me that He is releasing fresh manna and hidden mysteries in these last days. The only way you will know this is through the Holy Spirit. This is the only way you will be able to comprehend the end time moves of God.

The enemy will still be giving out old stale outdated bread which will have nothing to do with the end time moves of God. He can't know or understand them because they are spiritually discerned. So stay close to the Spirit of God in this hour and look for and decide if you want to eat of fresh manna or stale bread?

Colossians 1:26 [Amplified]

The mystery of which was hidden for ages and generations [from angels and men], but is now revealed to His holy people (the saints),

I Corinthians 2:5

That your faith should not stand in the wisdom of men, but in the power of God.

I Corinthians 2:7

But we speak the wisdom of God in a mystery, even the hidden wisdom, which God ordained before the world unto our glory:

I Corinthians 2:8a

Which none of the princes of this world knew:

The Fix It Man

Once in a vision I saw a man dressed all in white with a tool belt on and he had a flashlight in his hand. Behind him was his truck and written on the side of the truck were the words – Fix It Man. Now, he was standing on the outside of a dark underground garage and was looking around with his flashlight when he spotted something. So I asked, "What is he doing?"

Then the Lord asked me, "What do you see?"

So I said, "I see a man with a flashlight looking into a dark garage and there is a truck behind him."

Then the Lord said, "This is how you should be, out looking into dark places with the light of Christ, ready to put your tools to use and to know that all of Heaven is behind you."

St. Matthew 5:16
[16] Let your light so shine before men, that they may see your good works, and glorify your Father which is in heaven.

Angels Driving Dump Trucks

In the beginning of 2011 our church went on a corporate fast. During this time the Lord revealed to our pastor that He was giving us a fresh start and a new beginning. During this same period of time, God had given me a vision where I saw angels in mid air driving dump trucks.

I asked the Lord, "What are they doing?"

He said, "They are collecting debris of sins and transgressions."

I asked, "Where are they taking them?"

And He said, "To the sea of forgetfulness."

Hebrews 8:12

For I will be merciful to their unrighteousness, and their sins and their iniquities I will remember no more."

Isaiah 43:25
"I, even I, am He who blotteth out thy transgressions for Mine own   sake;
And I will not remember your sins."

Micah 7:19

He will turn again, He will have compassion upon us; He will subdue our iniquities; and thou will cast all their sins into the depths of the sea.

Knock, Knock, Who's There?

I began to hear knocking and ringing. These were so real to me that I would actually pick up the phone and say hello or go to the front door to ask who was there. Now I would answer them no matter the time, day or night or whatever I was doing, I would stop and answer them.

Then one day I asked the Lord, "Why do I hear this knocking and ringing and then when I answer them, no one is there?"

A few days later He answered me and said, "Whatever you are doing, no matter the time, day or night, you will stop and answer them."

Then He said, "This is how I want you to be with me, no matter what you are doing or the time if it is day or night, stop and answer me!"

And so I do, only now I know when I hear, Knock, Knock who's there. Amen.

Revelation 3:20

Behold, I stand at the door, and knock: if any man hear my voice, and open the door, I will come in to him, and will sup with him, and he with me.

The Bird and the Fish

Once, in a dream, I was in a certain place. I don't know what this place was. All I knew was that Jesus was there and I was so excited about seeing Him. But, all these other people were there and just as excited to see Him and they surrounded Him.

Now, these men and women of God had done great things and I thought to myself as I began to back away, how will Jesus ever know that I am here when all of these great men and women are here? I felt so alone and so small. Broken hearted, I turned to walk away when suddenly I was a little bird flying alone in the sky. Then I was a little fish swimming alone in a big ocean.

Then the Lord spoke and said, "You may feel like a little bird flying alone but I am the big sky watching over you. And, you may seem like a little fish swimming alone, but I am the big ocean surrounding you."

Then He said, "Barbara, I am aware of you every second of the day and you have my utmost attention, I am always with you." Then just as suddenly I realized that I was still at the same place and with the same people and that Jesus knew that I too was there. Amen!

Psalm 139:7

Whither shall I go from thy spirit? or whither shall I flee from thy presence?

Psalm 139:8a

If I ascend up into heaven, thou art there

Psalm 139:9

If I take the wings of the morning, and dwell in the uttermost parts of the sea;

Psalm 139:17a

How precious also are thy thoughts unto me, O God! how great is the sum of them!

Psalm 139:7

If I should count them, they are more in number than the sand: when I awake, I am still with thee

Moving Forward

I was in the presence of the Father and an angel moved out in front of me. His movements were as if someone was gently flipping through the pages of a book. When he moved forward the rest of him gently came into him.

Then, the Father spoke and said: "Know this. As surely as I have said that something is going to take place in your life, it already has. The rest of you just has to catch up with it."

Jeremiah 1:4 – 5

Then the word of the LORD came unto me, saying: Before I formed thee in the belly I knew thee; and before thou camest forth out of the womb I sanctified thee, and I ordained thee a prophet unto the nations.

The Angel and the Compass

I saw in a vision an angel standing in mid air over the sea. Under his feet was a compass and inside of the compass was a cross. But before I could ask the Lord what it meant, I heard the angel say in a loud clarion voice:

"Go ye the way of the cross!"

St. Matthew 10:38

And he that taketh not his cross, and followeth after me, is not worthy of me.

The sea represented the people of God, the compass the way they should go. The cross represented suffering.

The Trained Eye

On one occasion the Lord asked me this question, "What makes good art?"

I answered, "I don't know."

Then, the Lord went on to say, "It is not always how beautiful something looks. Sometimes good art can look strange; but to the trained eye, it is a masterpiece."

He continued, "Train your spiritual eye because sometimes the things that look the most beautiful could be rejected by me. And what looks different and strange could be me at work creating a Masterpiece!"

St. Matthew 3:4

And the same John had his raiment of camel's hair, with a leather girdle around his waist; and his meat was locusts and wild honey

St. Matthew 23:27

"Woe to you, scribes and Pharisees, hypocrites! For you are like unto whited sepulchers which indeed appear beautiful outwardly, but are within full of dead men's bones and all uncleanness".

St. Matthew 23:28

Even so ye also outwardly appear righteous unto men, but within are full of hypocrisy and iniquity.

The Donkey and the Horse

While talking with the Lord about horses, and how much I would like to ride one with Him, He gave me a vision of a donkey and a horse standing side by side.

So I asked Him, "What does this mean?"

He said, "You don't know enough about the donkey to be ready for the horse. There is suffering a hardness and humility that come with riding the donkey that can help to prepare you not only to ride, but to run with the horses."

Then he said, "Barbara, I came in on a donkey, but I'm coming back on a horse!"

St. Matthew 21:5

Tell ye the daughter of Sion, Behold, thy King cometh unto thee, meek, and sitting upon an ass, and a colt the foal of an ass.

Revelation 19:11

And I saw heaven opened, and behold a white horse; and he that sat upon him was called Faithful and True, and in righteousness he doth judge and make war.

The Chess Game

In a vision I was in a room with the devil – playing chess and the room was filled with demons and it appeared as if I was losing the game. Then Jesus walked into the room and sat down next to me. He began to play for me. As the game progressed, it looked as if the Lord was losing too. All I heard was the devil saying, "Check, check, check." The demons were excited and getting louder and louder.

Then Jesus, with one swift move said, "Check Mate!" At that, every demon left, and the devil disappeared. Amen

I Corinthians 15:57 [Amplified]

But thanks be to God, Who gives us the victory [making us conquerors] through our Lord Jesus Christ.

II Corinthians 2:14

Now thanks be unto God, which always causeth us to triumph in Christ,

Colossians 2:15

And having spoiled principalities and powers, he made a shew of them openly, triumphing over them in it.

The Golf Bag

Once I asked the Lord, "Why do I keep letting certain things get to me?"

Then, in a vision I saw a golf bag with clubs in it and the Lord said, "I am going to teach you something about golf." I thought to myself, golf, what's that got to do with anything?

He went on to say, "The object of the game is to get the ball into the hole with as few strokes as possible. This game requires practice, skill, and know-how. Learn how and why certain things keep affecting you the way they do. And then, just like in golf, with practice skill and know how you can shoot a hole in one and move on from that place. But remember the vision, if the irons stay in the bag then nothing will happen."

Deuteronomy 2:2-3

And the LORD spake unto me, saying, Ye have compassed this mountain long enough: turn you northward

THE END

The Lord showed me the words THE END as in a movie when it ends and shows who got credit for the work that had been done, like: sound, music, lights, right down to the minutest detail, someone received credit for it.

So I asked the Lord, "What in the world is this and what could it possibly mean?"

He answered and said, "At the end of your life's story on this earth, who will get the credit for the work you have done? Make sure that the work that you do is for the Glory of God! And not for your own glory!"

St. John 17:4

I have glorified thee on the earth. I have finished the work which thou gavest Me to do.

The Lion Kings

In a vision I saw lions sitting on thrones with crowns on their heads, but, sucking their thumbs. So I asked God, "What is this?"

He answered, "This is how they look when they are first called. They don't have a clue as to who they really are."

But as I watched they began to transform. They took on a new resolve and mind set. As they became partakers of Christ, they became fierce and regal looking. They sat as kings over realms and galaxies and knew who they now were in Christ, and I watched as they became like Jesus the true Lion King!

Hebrews 3:14

For we are made partakers of Christ, if we hold the beginning of our confidence steadfast unto the end;

Revelation 5:5

And one of the elders saith unto me, Weep not: behold, the Lion of the tribe of Judah, the Root of David, hath prevailed to open the book, and to loose the seven seals thereof.

I John 3:2

Beloved, now are we the sons of God, and it doth not yet appear what we shall be: but we know that, when he shall appear, we shall be like him; for we shall see him as he is.

Metamorphosized by Trial

A dear sister and friend in the Lord went through a lot of hardships and sufferings. Then, the Lord gave me a vision in which I saw her wrapped from her head to her feet. Horrified! I asked the Lord, "What is this and why is she bound like this?"

Then He said, "She is not bound in the way you suppose. I Love her, and I am metamorphosizing her."

Romans 8:18

For I reckon that the sufferings of this present time are not worthy to be compared with the glory which shall be revealed in us.

II Corinthians 4:17

For our light afflictions, which is but for a moment worketh for us a far more exceeding and eternal weight of glory.

I Peter 5:10
But the God of all grace who has called us into eternal glory by Christ Jesus, after that ye have suffered awhile, make you perfect, established, strengthened, settle you.

Spirit and Flesh

I was riding past a patch of land. As I looked I saw how hard and dry the land was. Then suddenly, in a vision, I was in a boat on this patch of dry land trying with all of my might to row.

As hard as I tried it only moved one inch Backward! Then, just as suddenly the dry land turned into a body of water. As I rowed in the water every stroke was made with ease.

Then I heard the voice of the Lord say, "This is the difference between being in the flesh and flowing in His Spirit."

Dry dirt = Flesh.
Water = Spirit.

Galatians 5:17

For the flesh lusteth against the Spirit, and the Spirit against the flesh: and these are contrary the one to the other: so that ye cannot do the things that ye would.

The Octopus

Once while dealing with a number of different hardships and trials (all at the same time) I saw myself in a vision wrestling with an octopus. I fought with all of my might and was only freed from one of its arms. I was completely wiped out.

That was when the Lord spoke and asked, "What are you going to do?" You are wiped out already and still have seven more arms to go."

I said, "Lord, I don't know, I am so tired of this battle."

Then the Lord spoke again and said, "If you kill the root cause which is the head; then the other seven arms will automatically die."

I Corinthians 10:13

There hath no temptation taken you but such as is common to man: but God is faithful who will not suffer you to be tempted above that ye are able, but will with the temptation also make a way to escape, that you may be able to bear it.

Deuteronomy 28:7

The LORD shall cause thine enemies that rise up against thee to be smitten before thy face: they shall come out against thee one way, and flee before thee seven ways.

The Rooster and the Bride

I saw in a vision a rooster and a bride. So I asked the Lord, "What does this mean?

And He said, "The rooster symbolizes the dawning of a new day, and the bride, the Lord's wife." He continued, "There is a new day dawning for the Bride. She is being transitioned, and she is on the brink of something that has never been seen or heard before."

God is getting ready to do a new thing with His bride.

Isaiah 43:19a

Behold, I will do a new thing; now it shall spring forth; shall ye not know it? I will even make a way in the wilderness, and rivers in the desert.

Acts 13:41

Behold, ye despisers, and wonder, and perish: for I work a work in your days, a work which ye shall in no wise believe, though a man declare it unto you.

The Biting and Devouring Church

Once in a vision I saw a beautiful church, so I went in and the people in pews were all dressed up and looking very nice. Smiles were on every face as they nodded and greeted one another.

Then, in a blink of an eye, the people turned into animals and I saw lions biting on sheep, bears were tearing at deer and leopards biting on the necks of giraffes. Then, to my amazement, I saw a weasel run down the middle of the aisle and stand behind the pulpit.

Then, in a snap, things were back as they were before with those smiling faces. The Lord spoke and said, "This is how they appear in the natural, but I have shown you what they are really like in their spirits, and they are indicative of my church."

Galatians 5:15

But if ye bite and devour one another, take heed that ye be not consumed one of another

The Captain and the Pilot

I had a vision of me on the seashore looking out at the ocean when I saw a speed boat come straight at me. When I looked at the man steering the boat I saw that He was Jesus! Then He said to me, "Hop in." Climbing in I thought to myself if I were to see Him in a boat I would think it would look like a boat from biblical days. Then He said, "Barbara, those would be too slow."

The next thing I knew we were flying swiftly in an airplane and then He said, "Things are quickly accelerating, racing swiftly toward the end. If you will allow me to be the Captain and the Pilot of your soul; I will navigate you through the turbulent times ahead and get you safely home.

Revelation 22:20

He which testifieth these things saith, Surely I come quickly. Amen. Even so, come, Lord Jesus.

A Generation

I saw roadside equipment by the side of a road that needed a lot of work. But suddenly the equipment began to turn on each other, and before long there was just a pile of junk and my heart was broken because I knew some how that this road led to Jesus. So I asked the Lord, "What is this?"

And He answered, "This is symbolic of the church that is still bickering over religion, teachings, and doctrines."

So I asked Him, "What can be done?"

Then He said, "Look over there," and as I turned, I saw brand new shiny equipment coming over the horizon. They worked in harmony and were purposefully driven. They moved the old equipment out of the way and got the work finished in no time.

Then He said, "There is a generation coming!"

Psalm 24:6

This is the generation [description] of those who seek Him [who inquire of and for Him and of necessity require Him], who seek Your face, [O God of] Jacob. Selah [pause, and think of that]!

Psalm 102:18

This shall be written for the generation to come: and the people which shall be created shall praise the LORD

Peter 2:9

But ye are a chosen generation, a royal priesthood, an holy nation, a peculiar people; that ye should shew forth the praises of him who hath called you out of darkness into his marvellous light;

Psalm 22:30

A seed shall serve Him; it shall be accounted to the Lord for a generation.

The Arrow and the Trumpet

I saw in a vision a great angel – large and very strong. The angel was holding a bow and arrow. He was dressed as an archer and had his bow drawn back and ready to shoot. Above him I saw another angel clothed in a white flowing robe with a trumpet up to his lips, poised to blow it, but did not. I could not see what the angel with the bow and arrow was aiming at, but it was certain that he would hit his mark. However, he could not move until he heard the sound of the trumpet.

So I asked the Lord, "What does this mean?"

He replied, "The angels cannot move until the church does, and she's about to!"

Zechariah 9:14

Then the LORD will be seen over them, And His arrow will go forth like lightning. The Lord GOD will blow the trumpet, And go with whirlwinds from the south.

Zechariah 9:15

The LORD of hosts shall defend them;

The Three Mes'

The Lord appeared to me and turned into this huge eagle. The next thing I knew I was on his back and we were flying toward this huge majestic mountain. Now, the closer we got to the mountain I could see two figures. One was on the very top and one was on the bottom. As we got closer still I could see that both of these figures were me.

Amazed! I said, "Lord, they are me." Then I asked, "How can I be at the top of the mountain and at the bottom of the mountain at the same time?"

Then, He answered, and said, "If you stay humble, and abased, I will exalt you spiritually.

I Peter5:6

Humble yourselves therefore under the mighty hand of God, that he may exalt you in due time:

Flesh, Blood and Steel

Once in a vision I saw a man whose hands, feet, and mouth were bound by something that looked strange to me. As I got closer I could see that it was skin. stonished! I asked the Lord, "What is this?"

He answered, "Because of the sin in this man's life he is bound by his own flesh. And Barbara, being bound by your flesh is stronger than any chains of steel."

So I asked, "How then can he be freed?"
Jesus answered, "Only by the Blood."

Romans 7:24

O wretched man that I am! who shall deliver me from the body of this death?

Romans 7:25a Amplified

O thank God! [He will!] through Jesus Christ (the Anointed One) our Lord!

Ephesians 1:7

In whom we have redemption through his blood,

Proverbs 5:22

His own iniquities shall take the wicked himself, and he shall be holden with the cords of his sins.

From the Foolishness to the Glory of the Cross

After time in prayer, I had a quick vision of the Lord hanging on the cross dressed as a court jester with a tear rolling down His cheek. Astonished, I asked the Lord, "What is this? Why are you dressed like that and crying?"

He said, "This is the Foolishness of the cross to so many of my people who refuse to believe that I lived, suffered, and died for their sins." Then He said, "Pray that their eyes will be opened, and their minds enlightened to understand the Glory of the Cross before it is too late."

I Corinthians 1:18a

For the preaching of the cross is to them that perish foolishness;

Galatians 6:14a

But God forbid that I should glory, save in the cross of our Lord Jesus Christ,

Keep Knocking

Once in a vision I saw Jesus standing at a door knocking. Now, I knew that the door represented me, so I asked the Lord, "Why are you knocking? I have already accepted you and have let you in."

He answered, "You have, but there are still doors inside of you that are closed to me. I am going to knock and keep knocking until you have opened every one to me, and I totally possess you."

And I replied, "Lord, Keep knocking."

Galatians 2:20

I am crucified with Christ: nevertheless I live; yet not I, but Christ liveth in me: and the life which I now live in the flesh I live by the faith of the Son of God, who loved me, and gave himself for me.

The Locomotive Pastor

Once while in prayer my pastor began to speak prophetically and moved us into a realm in the Spirit that changed the atmosphere. Then in a vision I saw a train, and how that everyone there began to connect like railroad cars. The pastor was the engine and the smoke of the Holy Spirit was all around him. He was pulsating with the power of the Holy Spirit. You could actually feel it and I knew that we were being taken to a new place in prayer that we had never been before, but we had to stay connected.

Then, Jesus, like an engineer of a train, went through each compartment stamping us. Then the vision ended. But He left me with this – if we stay connected and on one accord, He will lead us to places in prayer that we have never been before.

Romans 8:26 [Amplified]

So too the [Holy] Spirit comes to our aid *and* bears us up in our weakness; for we do not know what prayer to offer *nor* how to offer it worthily as we ought, but the Spirit Himself goes to meet our supplication *and* pleads in our behalf with unspeakable yearnings *and* groanings too deep for utterance.

Romans 8:27 [Amplified]

And He Who searches the hearts of men knows what is in the mind of the [Holy] Spirit [what His intent is], because the Spirit intercedes *and* pleads [before God] in behalf of the saints according to *and* in harmony with God's will.

The Sword of the Cross

In a vision, the Lord gave me a sword. Now, He had given me other swords in the past; swords of gold, fire and one made of light. But this sword as soon as I saw it I was heartbroken. It was made of old wood and held together by a piece of old rope.

Saddened, I asked, "Was this because I hadn't used the others skillfully enough?"

He answered, "Barbara, this is the most powerful weapon in your arsenal. It is a part of the Cross, and is stained in my blood. You won't need to fight with this sword; all you'll have to do is lift it up."

Exodus 14:16

But lift thou up thy rod, and stretch out thine hand over the sea, and divide it: and the children of Israel shall go on dry ground through the midst of the sea

Exodus 14:14

The LORD shall fight for you, and ye shall hold your peace

Exodus 14:26

And the LORD said unto Moses, Stretch out thine hand over the sea, that the waters may come again upon the Egyptians, upon their chariots, and upon their horsemen.

The Wind Up Dolls

Once in a vision I saw baby saints like wind up dolls. They were bumping into walls, doors and each other. So I asked God what was wrong with them.

He said, "They have been saved but left with no direction or guidance." Then He said,   "Don't get them saved and then just leave them."

"Direct Them!
Guide Them!
 Feed Them!"

"Equip them to go forth and to enlarge the kingdom."

Acts 20:28

Take heed therefore unto yourselves, and to all the flock, over the which the Holy Ghost hath made you overseers, to feed the church of God, which he hath purchased with his own Blood.

Making Holes Whole

While praying for my pastor, I saw in a vision her suddenly turn into a large knitting needle. Then I looked out over the congregation and saw holes in different parts of peoples' spirits, souls and bodies. Then I saw her begin to move with acceleration, mending those holes. Some were hurts, sicknesses, confusion, sadness and spiritual blindness. But she was busy at work making all those holes, whole. Amen!

Hole: A hollow and empty place.

Whole: Complete, restored and sound.

I Thessalonians 5:23

And the very God of peace sanctify you wholly; and I pray God your whole spirit and soul and body be preserved blameless unto the coming of our Lord Jesus Christ

The Closet

Once, in a vision, I was with the Lord and saw a very large closet. I went inside and saw all these ministerial tools there. So I got very busy organizing - putting things here and there, using this and that. I got so caught up in the work that I hardly noticed Jesus anymore.

Then I realized that as I worked, it got darker and darker. The work became more and more tedious and I wasn't utilizing the tools effectively anymore. Then I looked up and saw only a slither of light coming through the door, and the door was closing, with Jesus on the other side. So, I jumped up and ran out – just as the door closed.

Then the Lord spoke to me and said, "Don't let even ministry separate you from me."

St. Luke 10:40a

But Martha was cumbered about much serving, and came to him

St. Luke 10:41
And Jesus answered and said unto her, Martha, Martha, thou art careful and troubled about many things:

St. Luke 10:42

But one thing is needful: and Mary hath chosen that good part, which shall not be taken away from her.

The Light of Day

The Lord spoke to me and said, "Barbara, light doesn't shine in the daylight - only at night." Then He said, "In a room full of Christians it is day. But in a room full of sinners it is dark and that is where your light shines best – so, go out and shine."

St. Matthew 5:14

Ye are the light of the world. A city that is set on an hill cannot be hid.

St. Matthew 5:15

Neither do men light a candle, and put it under a bushel, but on a candlestick; and it giveth light unto all that are in the house.

St. Matthew 5:16

Let your light so shine before men, that they may see your good works, and glorify your Father which is in heaven.

Is Not This The Carpenter?

In a vision I saw a man dressed as a carpenter, working on something unusual, certainly something I had never seen before. As I got closer I saw that the man was Jesus. He turned and said, "I am the Carpenter."

Turning back to his work with a wink and a smile He said, "Just wait and see what I have prepared for you."

St. John 14:2 -3

In my Father's house are many mansions: if it were not so, I would have told you. I go to prepare a place for you.

St. John 14:3

And if I go and prepare a place for you, I will come again, and receive you unto myself; that where I am, there ye may be also.

St. Mark 6:3

Is not this the carpenter?

The Flip Side of the Narrow Way

The Lord spoke to me and said, "As you continue on this journey with me, the way will become narrower and narrower. But the wider, broader, and more range you will have in the Spirit realm even to the Throne of God!"

St. Matthew 7:14

Because strait is the gate, and narrow is the way, which leadeth unto life, and few there be that find it.

2 Peter 1:11

For so an entrance shall be ministered unto you abundantly into the everlasting kingdom of our Lord and Saviour Jesus Christ.

The Pioneer

Once in a vision I saw myself sitting in a covered wagon looking out over a plain. But this was no earthly plain. It was more like spiritual plains, realms and dimensions.

Then I heard the voice of the Lord say, "Dare to go where few have ever gone before."

Ezekiel 3:22

And the hand of the LORD was there upon me; and he said unto me, Arise, go forth into the plain, and I will there talk with thee.

Ezekiel 3:23a

[23] Then I arose, and went forth into the plain: and, behold, the glory of the LORD stood there,

Finding Gold

The Lord said, "Taking counsel from the ungodly is like following a bread crumb trail - at the end there is a trap. But the counsel of the godly is like following a rainbow, at the end of the rainbow, you will always find gold."

Psalm 1:1a

Blessed is the man that walketh not in the counsel of the ungodly,

Psalm 1:3

And he shall be like a tree planted by the rivers of water, that bringeth forth his fruit in his season; his leaf also shall not wither; and whatsoever he doeth shall prosper.